Meher Baba

LIFE AT ITS BEST

By Meher Baba

EDITED BY IVY O. DUCE

Second Printing February 1964
Third Printing November 1969
Perennial Library Edition Published 1972
Fourth Printing June 1974

Library of Congress Catalog Card Number: 57-14432
Printed in the United States of America
Connecticut Printers, Inc.

Address of Sufism Reoriented, Inc.
1290 Sutter Street, San Francisco, CA 94109

The Contents

2177551

THE GOAL (SELF-REALIZATION) AND ITS ATTAINMENT

GENERAL MESSAGES TO MANKIND

MEHER BABA AND HIS ACTIVITIES

He who knows everything
displaces nothing.
To each one I appear to be
what he thinks I am.

FOREWORD

Dr. W. Y. Evans-Wentz

This small, but precious, volume of American-born messages from Meher Baba, the illustrious Sadguru of India, should prove to be, not only to his own disciples, but to all pilgrims who have entered upon the Path, a source of unending inspiration. Every such book adds, in its own peculiar way, to the spiritual heritage of our One Humanity, and thereby advances Right Knowledge, not only in this generation, but in all generations yet to come.

These messages constitute an authentic record of Meher Baba's transcendent thought as he traveled across the United States, meeting his many followers, during three weeks of the summer of 1956, and observed the complex phantasmagoria of life in that part of the world. All the while still strictly maintaining his silence, which has now been unbroken for thirty-two years, the Teacher delivered the messages by means of hand gestures rather than with the aid of his alphabet board.

Much that Meher Baba observed then in America seems to have served, metaphorically, for the setting forth of his teachings. This is suggested by the section entitled "Theory and Practice," on page 23, where he likens spiritually undirected thinking, talking and writing to the steam which escapes through the whistle of a railway engine. The whistling makes a noise, but no amount of it can set the engine in motion. Only by a different application of its steam can the engine with its train attain a distant destination. Likewise, without wisely directed discipline there can be no spiritual progress. Mere theorizing will never advance the disciple; it is practice, not theory, that produces results. This yogic truism is further emphasized on page 52 in "Knowledge Through Experience"; and, also, in a more subtle manner, on page 37 in "Tuition and Intuition." On page 23, the differences between the slow goods train, and the oft-stopping ordinary passenger train, and the special train are cleverly applied to the three classes of devotees.

One of the most original of these metaphorical applications is set forth on page 25, in "Humility Disarms Antagonism": the disciple when meeting with aggression "should be like the football that is kicked, for the very kicking raises it aloft and propels it onward till the goal is reached." The late Mahatma Gandhi, too, would say, as Meher Baba in this context does, "True humility is strength, not weakness. It disarms antagonism and ultimately conquers it." Once the leaders of the nations see that this is so, human warfare will be ended.

"Control," on page 26, very succinctly, in sixty-six words, expounds the whole essence of applied yoga. No wiser definition of the term God has ever been formulated than that set forth on page 13:

Philosophers, atheists and others may affirm or refute the existence of God, but as long as they do not deny the existence of their own being they continue to testify to their belief in God — for I tell you, with divine authority, that God is Existence, eternal and infinite. He is EVERYTHING.

As Einstein mathematically demonstrated, energy and matter equal one another; and now Meher Baba enunciates, in "Control of Mind Over Energy and Matter," on page 38, that energy and matter are begotten of mind, a truth towards which Western Science appears to be rapidly advancing.

Of the many golden precepts contained herein, the three which follow suffice to indicate the profundity of their author's insight: —

It is not so much that you are within the cosmos as that the cosmos is within you.

The saints of the present are the sinners of the past.

While wine leads to self-oblivion, Divine Love leads to self-knowledge.

In the firm conviction that the fifty-eight messages of Meher Baba, which comprise this volume, will be found to be, as has been said of the messages of Tibet's Great Yogi Milarepa, "a feast of delight to them who uphold the Dynasty of Gurus by living according to their commandments," I conclude this Foreword with "The Final Account," on page 58:

When the goal of life is attained, one achieves the reparation of all wrongs, the healing of all wounds, the righting of all failures, the sweetening of all sufferings, the relaxation of all strivings, the harmonizing of all strife, the unraveling of all enigmas, and the real and full meaning of all life — past, present and future.

8

Life at Its Best

If understood, life is simply a jest;
If misunderstood, life becomes a pest.
Once overcome, life is ever at rest.
For pilgrims of the Path, life is a test.
When relinquished through love,
                                      life is at its best.

God and His Attributes

GOD'S DIVINE BUSINESS

GOD the everlasting and indivisible, transacts His universal illusory business of duality by playing His dual role of opposites simultaneously and eternally. Saints are God's assets and sinners are His liabilities. God, the infinite source of wisdom and justice, goes on eternally turning His liabilities into assets.

THE REAL GIFT

WHAT is meant by the "real gift"?

If a gift is to be real, then both the giver and receiver of the gift must forget the transaction completely. To forget completely would mean that the giver should not feel he has given, and the receiver should not know he has received. If the giver does not forget, then he has obligated the receiver; and if the receiver does not forget, he experiences a sense of obligation towards the giver. The real gift of love bestowed on man comes from God alone, and remembrance is absent in both the One who gives and the one who receives. Because of this complete forgetfulness man can strive eternally to love God, and God remains the eternal Beloved for mankind.

How can God, Who is omniscient, forget? Because unless He "forgets," the gift He bestows upon man cannot be the real gift that it is. Man, too, is left in ignorance of the operation of this gift, through which he ultimately realizes his Godhood.

When the Omniscient bestows the real gift of love, He manifests His complete forgetfulness of it by apparently becoming callous towards His lovers. Hence the untold sufferings on the path of love that are experienced by the lovers of God, as also the unimaginable pangs of separation felt by them for their only Beloved, God.

Because God is omniscient and knows the real meaning of the real gift, He becomes callous towards His lover who, absorbed in the profound depth of God's love, becomes oblivious that he loves Him and that it is a gift from Him, and hence loves Him ever more intensely.

It is this "forgetfulness" which arouses in the lover the unallayed pangs of separation and consumes him in the ever growing fires of this incomparable love from which he emerges in the image of his Beloved in triumphant and eternal unity.

GOD IS ETERNAL EXISTENCE

Philosophers, atheists and others may affirm or refute the existence of God, but as long as they do not deny the very existence of their own being they continue to testify to their belief in God—for I tell you with divine authority, that God is Existence, eternal and infinite. He is Everything.

Whether man knows it or not, there is for him only one aim in life, and eventually he realizes this when he consciously experiences his own eternal and infinite state of "I Am God."

GOD, MAN, AND THE GOD-MAN

The entire universe is God's shadow and belongs to God, but God does not belong to the universe. God's shadow comes out of God, undergoes infinite variations and goes back into God.

God's shadow depends upon God; God does not depend upon His shadow. Without God the shadow cannot exist. Without the shadow God does exist. God was when the universe was not. God is when the universe is. God will be when the universe will not be.

Your own shadow belongs to you but you need not belong to your shadow. Your shadow necessarily clings to you, but you unnecessarily cling to your shadow. Without you your shadow cannot exist, but without your shadow you do exist.

In all states and under all circumstances, whether you are dreaming dreams in sleep, dreaming the dream of life on earth, dreaming acute hell or heaven states after leaving the gross body, or dreaming the real dreams in the higher spiritual planes, essentially you remain the same. Everything and everyone represents God in one way or another, in some state of consciousness or another — but the God-Man (Avatar, Buddha, Christ, Rasool) represents God in every way, in everything, and everywhere, in one and all of the states of consciousness, manifest or latent.

Hafiz, the man who became God-realized, says:

Jehān-o-kāré jehān, jumla heech der heech ast,
Hazār bār mun in nukta karda-am tehqiqe.

"A thousand times I have ascertained and found it to be true that the universe and the affairs of the universe are totally nothing into nothing."

GOD KNOWS NOT, TO GOD KNOWS SELF

As ORDINARY man, when God knows not He is God, for all time His imagination remains the universe and Self remains imaginary.

As the Perfect One, when man becomes God and ceases to remain anything else, for all time and beyond time His imagination disappears and He remains SELF-conscious.

As a Perfect Master, when man becomes God and knows He has been man, for all time His creation remains imagination and He remains SELF-conscious.

As God-Man, when God becomes man and knows He is God, for the time being His imagination becomes everything and for all time and beyond time He remains SELF-conscious.

The Master and His Role

DEATHLESS LIVING

LIFE does not end with death. Survival after death is as true as death after life. To live in order to die, or to die in order to survive, would be a poor proposition indeed. The death that follows life is not a lifelessness, nor is life after death a deathlessness. Life is a positive manifestation of the true Existence which negative death cannot extinguish. To end the ceaseless succession of lives and deaths, death itself has to be annihilated *in life*. On annihilating death in life by completely freeing consciousness of all illusion, man becomes God in the naked truth of His own true existence. He remains infinitely conscious God, irrespective of His keeping or dropping the gross, subtle and mental bodies, just as man remains man whether he is dressed or undressed.

As long as man remains ignorant of his divine Self he may as well be a stone; a man lives and a stone exists, and both remain equally ignorant of the Truth. As Kabir says, while man cannot achieve TRUTH he is no better than a stone.

Man's full consciousness, painstakingly earned through the endless illusory experiences during evolution, is trapped within these very experiences that were so necessary to enable him to gain the consciousness achieved. In man, consciousness is complete. Augmenting of consciousness is no longer needed, but merely the directing of it towards man's *real* identity.

Only in the human form is it possible for life to attain its final goal, which is to realize the all-pervading and infinite Divinity. Only in the human body can one attain realization and fulfill the purpose of creation. Hence the supreme importance of attaining the human body.

For all practical purposes, attaining the human body is the journey's end, but the *sanskaras* (impressions) amassed in the travail of gaining this consciousness block man's view of his eternal Self. All the suffering and struggles man undergoes are to wear out this obstruction, and this involves an interminable process. Man cannot of himself remove the block, but a Perfect Master can do that for him, when his grace is deserved.

THE LIMITING NIGHTMARE

THE process of getting bound and then un-
bound is charged with immense significance.
The soul gets mixed up with the body and then
gets caught up with it.

The soul is like a parrot and the body is like
a cage. When the parrot is outside of the cage
it is free, but it does not fully appreciate what
freedom is. Not having known confinement, it
does not recognize being outside of the cage as
"freedom." When it goes through encagement,
the agonizing bondage causes it to appreciate
what freedom really is. Then, when the parrot
is set free again, it truly enjoys its freedom.

The same thing happens to the soul, when,
through the grace of the Perfect Master, it is
freed from the limiting nightmare in which it
believes itself to be nothing but its own encag-
ing body.

DYNAMIC FREEDOM

THE unlimited freedom of the Truth-realized
person is the only real and full freedom. Only
in such dynamic freedom flowing through a

Perfect Master can the Self as Truth manifest Itself, thus expressing the divinized impressions of the universal mind. The divinized impressions are infinitely creative and efficient, because they are infinitely submissive to the Self. They release creative and divine action, which is unlimited.

But the ordinary binding impressions of the ego-mind are unendingly aggressive to the Self and seek their own fulfillment. They are thus infinitely limited in efficiency and creativity.

DIRECT JOURNEY TO GOD

THE masses who try to attain the Truth by following rites and rituals are, as it were, in the goods train which is detained indefinitely at various stations. Those who sincerely and devotedly meditate on God or dedicate their lives to the service of humanity are, as it were, in the ordinary train which stops at every station according to the time-table. But those who seek the company of the Truth-realized Master and carry out his orders in full surrenderance and faith are, as it were, in a special train which will take them to the goal in the shortest possible time, without halts at intermediate stations.

THE MASTER IS THE WAY

IN THINKING day and night of the Master, the disciple *nearly* achieves the ultimate objective which is the aim of the diverse practices of meditation and concentration. By putting the work of the Master above his own personal needs, he *achieves* the aim through complete renunciation.

In sincere surrender to the Master, the disciple comes *very* near to the stopping of the mind, which is the goal of most yogic processes. In obeying the Master at any cost and serving him selflessly, he *nearly* arrives at the culmination of the Path of understanding and action. And in loving the Master above everything else, he *becomes* one with the Master as Truth and thus attains Godhood — the goal of all search and endeavor — through his grace.

THE GRINDING MILL OF
THE UNIVERSE

THE Perfect Master becomes the center of the universe. He finds himself as the only absolute and changeless point, around which the entire universe is constantly turning. The universe is like the grinding mill, and the Truth-realized Master is like its central pin. None can escape the repetitive and eternal crushing that goes on in this grinding mill except those grains which adhere to the central pin.

THE FLASH FROM THE ETERNAL

THE act of a Perfect Master is not repetitive. It is not merely the re-doing of something previously experienced in the context of a new setting. It is the doing of something that can not be done within the restrictions of the experiences of duality. It is a creation of the utterly new, a descent of the Truth into the false. Hence its creativity is infinite. The redeeming act of a Perfect Master is a flash of the Eternal in the midst of what is otherwise nothing but rigidly determined causation. This is the mystery of divine grace bestowed by the Perfect Master.

The Disciple and His Attitudes

THEORY AND PRACTICE

THE energy which is expended in mere thinking, talking or writing is like the steam which escapes through the whistle of the railway engine. The whistle makes a noise, and is even interesting, but it cannot drive the engine. No amount of whistling can move the engine forward. The steam has to be harnessed and used intelligently in order that it may actually take the engine to its destination. That is why the sages have always insisted on practice rather than theory. This applies particularly to those who want to know and realize God.

THE IMMORTALITY OF UNIVERSAL LIFE

THE silence which I have been observing for the past thirty-one years is a call from the silence of unfathomable Divinity. Invite that Divinity into your hearts so that you may become permanently established in the immortality of universal life, which is vastly different from the persistence of limited individual life. The ego-life has a beginning and an end; the Truth which I bring is beginningless and endless. In order to inherit that Truth you need the courage to jump across the abyss of duality.

It is not possible to receive undying life in the Truth unless you surrender all resistance to it. You cannot drag along the prejudices of the past and yet hope to unfold Divinity within. You have to cut through the deposits of evolution and reincarnation and be completely receptive and susceptible to the lessons of life. If you meet life squarely, accepting its opposites with equanimity while carrying on your duties in a spirit of selfless love and service, you will not only come in tune with the Infinite, but you yourself will become the Infinite which you seek.

Learn the art of taking your stand on the Truth within. When you live in this Truth, the result is the fusion of the mind and the heart and the end of all fears and sorrow. It is not a dry attainment of mere power or intellectual knowledge. A love which is illumined by the intuitive wisdom of the spirit will bless your life with ever-renewing fulfillment and never-ending sweetness.

HUMILITY DISARMS ANTAGONISM

FOR real spiritual service the disciple has to be prepared for all eventualities. In his work for God he must learn to adjust himself to all types of circumstances — favorable or otherwise. Others may pay no heed to him or may treat him with contempt or slander, but that should not mar his understanding or sincerity. He should remain unmoved by all this and resist the onslaught of worldly opposition with true humility. When met with aggression he should be like the football that is kicked, for the very kicking raises it aloft and propels it onward till the goal is reached.

For the disciple, failure lies in betraying the Truth, not in accepting worldly abuse. Unwavering loyalty to the Truth of his search leads him on to the higher sphere of the unlimited divine life of real fulfillment. True humility is strength, not weakness. It disarms antagonism and ultimately conquers it.

HYPOCRISY

THERE is a demoralizing cleavage between what man is and what he wishes to appear to be. When hypocrisy comes into play it works much greater havoc within one's own psyche than in the outer sphere. The perceptible damage in the outer sphere is great, but the unperceived damage in the spiritual realm is stupendous.

The truth of one's own perception and realization is the only road by which wholeness may be restored to the inner psychic being. In no other way can man obtain release from the chains that tie the limited ego-mind to the colossal cosmic illusion which hides from him the perennial spring of the Divinity within.

CONTROL

KEEP your mind quiet, steady and firm. Do not submit to desires, but try to control them. One who cannot restrain his tongue cannot restrain his mind; one who cannot restrain his mind cannot restrain his action; one who cannot restrain his actions cannot restrain himself; and one who cannot restrain himself cannot attain his real Infinite Self.

SUPREMACY OF LIVING WISDOM

THE established codes of religion and morality are to mankind as is the general advice given by a father to his son. They are for its well-being. But when one may have the advantage of living wisdom, it should be accepted in preference to these established codes. This may be done not only without coming to harm, but with much benefit.

As stated by a Seer, wealth may be sacrificed for health, wealth and health for self-respect, and all three (wealth, health and self-respect) for one's own religion, but to gain God everything, including religion, should be sacrificed without hesitation.

The Self, Ego and Bindings

THE UMBRELLA OF MENTAL IMPRESSIONS

IN ACTUALITY, God is not far from the seeker, nor is it impossible to see Him. He is like the sun, which is ever shining right above you. It is you who have held over your head the umbrella of your variegated mental impressions which hide Him from your view. You have only to remove the umbrella and the Sun is there for you to see. It does not have to be brought there from anywhere. But such a tiny and trivial thing as an umbrella can deprive you of the sight of such a stupendous fact as the Sun.

THE IGNORANCE OF THE SEPARATIVE EGO

ANY thought, feeling or action which savors of the separative ego springs from unqualified ignorance. It is not a form of ignorance that one may

28

comfortably wear, or not wear, like an overcoat. It is an ignorance that binds. It is an ignorance that commits the self to unrelieved and degrading suffering, not necessarily of the physical body, but always and inevitably of the spirit. It is an ignorance attendant upon the betrayal of Truth and is, therefore, a form of self-betrayal.

It admits of no superficial and temporary remedies or bedridden compromises. It is an ignorance which shuts the soul from love and beauty, joy and freedom, conscious divinity and true Self-fulfillment. It is an ignorance which persists like a thorn in the flesh unless it is uprooted by complete acceptance of the Truth.

WRONG PERSPECTIVE

WRONG perspective must give wrong results. It is not correct to look upon the one Reality as being intended solely for any one manifestation of Itself. It is more accurate to look upon each and every manifestation as being intended for the one Reality. This means that the ego-centered point of view has to be surrendered in order to appreciate and know the Truth. God does not exist for one form or one religion. All forms and religions exist for God.

CREATIONS OF THE LIMITED MIND

MIND, which is subject to dispositional and impressional determinism, seeks and creates an over-powering false world, becomes enmeshed in it, and projects into it a false value that must in the end, due to its very nature, betray itself. Mind divides a reality which is essentially indivisible. It clings to a form which is essentially perishable. It glorifies itself in actions which are essentially binding and in achievements which are essentially insignificant. It enjoys and suffers against a background of vacuity, thus depriving itself of any real happiness or understanding.

The only way to live in the sanity of undeluded understanding is to become aware of this impressional determinism of the ego-mind and to become free of its vitiating constraint.

THE BINDING PAST

MAN is inescapably caught up in the flow of time and is under the pressing burden of the past which impels him now one way, now another. The past leaves its effect in the different spheres of existence and persists as a determinant factor which has to be reckoned with in the present.

Of all the accumulations of the past, those with the most far-reaching influence are the memories and habits that get settled in the mind as a by-product of the experiences to which it has been subjected. The limitations created by the hoary past (of the individual and mankind) have to be faced irrespective of their nature or intensity. However, they constitute a superfluous binding, as they pertain only to the manifestations of the spirit in creative history and not to its intrinsic being.

Another type of legacy of the past, which can bind the spirit vitally, consists in the shaping of human nature by the imprints and dispositions deposited in one's mind. One may try to run away from given circumstances and one may even have a certain measure of success in doing so; but one cannot run away from one's own mind.

The mind persists throughout life and also after death, on earth and in the states of heaven and hell, as well as in the endless succession of reincarnations. It is a never-failing companion of the individual soul and can never be annulled except in the state of liberation or realization.

From the spiritual point of view, the bindings created by the make-up of one's own mind are far more stupendous than the bindings created by external circumstances. Both types of bindings are the relics of the past and rigorously determine the experiences of the present and the possibilities of the future.

Man cannot act with true freedom in the present, because he drags with him his binding past. He goes on, inevitably creating suffering for himself and others, and also accumulating the self-created impressional or sanskaric momenta which constitute the fortresses of the limiting ego-mind. The past cannot be changed and has, as a chain of incidents, become petrified; but it continues to mold the present and shape the future of the limited "I."

REAL CHOICE

THE ego-mind feels and exercises its limited and illusory freedom when it chooses to succumb to one impressional disposition rather than another. It seems to enjoy freedom in and through its choice. But this freedom is only apparent; it is not freedom of choice. The impression has utilized the ego-mind in order to be released into expression. The ego-mind "chooses," but it has no real choice in choosing. Its choice is illusory.

The universal mind, on the contrary, feels and exercises unlimited freedom when it chooses to vivify and release any particular divinized impression. It has full freedom of choice. It may or may not choose to select a particular activity. Its choice is unlimited and real.

The ego-mind "chooses," but it chooses in ignorance and restricted freedom. The universal mind chooses, but it chooses in the knowledge of Truth and in unlimited freedom.

THE LAW OF KARMA

ALL things are governed by laws of one kind or another. Even insignificant business concerns and public institutions have their laws and cannot function without them. This is even more true of the universe. It may seem sometimes as if the universe were not subject to any self-justifying law, and sometimes it appears as if sincere toil were lost, the virtuous condemned to suffering and the vicious endowed with power and success. But this fractional and false view is derived from man's ignorance of the law of karma.

When the ego-mind refuses to understand life and encounters accumulated prejudices and resistance, it loses its equilibrium and tranquility. It is thus impelled either to release or inhibit good or bad actions, getting further involved in the results of its own activities, whether in the form of thoughts or deeds.

The law of karma prevents the ego-mind from escaping the results created by its own good or bad actions. The ego-mind is harnessed by the gathered momentum of past actions and is incapable of emancipation or true balance because it is constantly disturbed, not only by environmental knocks and impacts but also by the goadings of its own stored impressions. Although the ego-mind has an inherent tendency to keep restoring its lost equilibrium, it attempts such restoration through a mechanical reaction of going over to the opposite and clinging to that, until it discerns through experience that balance is not to be gained in such clinging either.

So the ego-mind goes from opposite to opposite in the illusory karmic pendulum until, through endless testing and suffering, it runs its course of opposite actions and reactions, or until it has the good fortune to contact a Perfect Master and receive his grace.

FREEDOM FROM OPPOSITES

EVERY man is subject to agreeable and disagreeable experiences — of pleasure and pain, success and failure, good and evil, wealth and poverty, power and helplessness, honor and dishonor, gain and loss, fulfillment and frustration.

Each of these opposites invites a suitable response in emotion or in action. Mind is moved by these opposites, and is continually losing its equilibrium and continually trying to restore it while constantly meeting the impacts of environmental changes.

During its various lives as a human being the ego-mind can oscillate endlessly between the opposites, *viz.*, indulgence and repression, secularism and religion, superiority complex and inferiority complex, self-aggrandizement and self-humiliation, introversion and extroversion, virtue and vice, pain and pleasure, "I" and "you" or "mine" and "thine," without arriving at true poise — attainable only through right understanding of the Truth. The oscillation of the ego-mind through the opposites is reactionary; therefore, though it passes through extremes it can not arrive at true poise.

True poise comes when the ego-mind, with all its accumulated inclinations, melts away through divine love, thus unveiling the supramental Truth in which there is the realization that one is — oneself — one with all life. Here there is no duality or division of life and therefore the soul is free from the opposite attitudes.

Having become one with the eternal and infinite divinity which sustains from within, the soul gains unending bliss, understanding, love and power, for the soul is free from duality.

CREATIVE AND AMPLIFICATORY IMPRINTS

Divinized imprints are not detractive but creative, not restrictive but amplificatory. Thus they are radically different from ego-prints. Essentially they are complementary assets added to the Universal Mind. Their function is not that of curtailment or restriction, but of supplementary increment. On the other hand, the binding impressions of the ego-mind are restrictive and detractive.

The difference between the binding impressions of the ego-mind and the divinized impressions of the Universal Mind is a difference in kind, not merely a difference of degree. In the same way, the difference between the freedom of the ego-mind and the freedom of the Universal Mind is not one of degree but of kind.

TUITION AND INTUITION

Intuition has been buried under the debris from the piecemeal tuition of the assailing experiences of the false. Tuition is impressed from without, while intuition dawns from within.

Tuition thwarts intuition. Therefore, the tutoring of the mind by external events has to be counteracted by inner awakening. Then and only then can intuition, in its transcendent understanding, truly judge without yielding to the stupor of indiscriminate impressibility.

CONTROL OF MIND OVER ENERGY AND MATTER

MIND begets energy and matter. Without mind there can be neither energy nor matter. Energy is derived from mind and is continually sustained by it; it cannot subsist without mind, latent or manifest. Matter depends upon energy and cannot remain matter without energy, latent or manifest.

Mind can subsist without energy, as energy can subsist without matter. In contrast to an infinite number of individual minds as completely separate entities from one another, the Universal Mind is indivisible and omnipresent.

Until mind achieves full control over all energy and matter, mind itself needs to be controlled. It must be protected against being swayed in the illusion of energy and matter, neither of which have even their illusory existence apart from mind. To control the mind from the effects and influence of energy and matter is very difficult. For example, when a man is slapped, his mind is apt to respond with an act of greater violence, and this action of revenge is an unnecessary distortion of the mind, a sheer waste of energy and fruitless use of matter.

Although some can achieve a partial and temporary control over their minds, very, very few through divine love can gain complete mastery over the mind and thus fully control all energy and matter. Eventually, divine love annihilates the very mind itself and then God, the divine Beloved, is realized.

THE IMPERISHABLE SWEETNESS

THE perennial spring of imperishable sweetness is within everyone. Yet, if man does not release that spring by removing the ego-blockade, he inevitably suffers in innumerable ways. All that lives is striving for happiness; yet a thousand and one pains and fears attend upon every pleasure which man seeks through the ignorance of exclusiveness.

All over the world, man buries himself in egoism and multicolored attachments to the false, depriving himself of the intrinsic and self-sustained happiness that does not wane. He seeks happiness through the perishing and transitional, and invites upon himself the sufferings of closed consciousness. One must contact the ocean of unfading bliss within, and be free of the limiting duality of "I" and "you," to unveil the perennial spring of imperishable sweetness which is within each and all.

The Goal (Self-realization) and Its Attainment

HAVE HOPE

THE modern era is steeped in restlessness as man is tossed between conflicting ideals. Like mounds in a sandy desert, intellectual knowledge is mounting up without provision for the expression of the heart, which is so vitally necessary to quench the need of the spirit. It is lack of this that has checkmated man's achievements, in spite of himself and his enormous advancements in the fields of science. Unhappiness and insecurity, emotional or otherwise, are the dominant notes of the age, and mankind is engulfed in the darkness of wars, hate and fear.

Yet I say, "Have hope."

Selfishness and lust for power tend to drag man towards brutality, which he has inherited from his evolutionary ancestry or acquired during erroneous searching through his incarnations. But there is within man the inextinguishable light of Truth, because he is essentially divine in origin and being.

Those who cleanse their hearts of the embittering poison of selfishness, hate and greed shall find God as their own true Self. When you find and realize God, the problem of selfishness and its numerous expressions melts away like mist before the sun. In God and as God, all life reveals itself as being really one and indivisible, and all separateness created by identification with human or sub-human forms is seen to be illusory.

The Truth of divine life is not a hope but a reality. It is the only reality, and all else is illusion. Have faith and you will be redeemed. Have love and you will conquer the lower and limited self of cravings that veil your own true being as God. Not through desperate self-seeking, but through constant self-giving is it possible to find the Self of all selves.

HAPPINESS AND BLISS

IF MAN wants the happiness he is striving for, let him be more aggressive towards himself and more tolerant towards others. This is no weakness or cowardice — it is the real strength of the brave. And if man wants to live eternally in bliss, let him live for God and be dead to his self.

✸

INTELLECTUAL PROOF

To ASK for a purely intellectual proof of the existence of God is like asking for the privilege of being able to see with your ears!

✸

VASTNESS OF THE SOUL

It DOES not require a large eye to see a large mountain. The reason is that, though the eye is small, the soul which sees through it is greater and vaster than all the things which it perceives. In fact, it is so great that it includes all objects, however large or numerous, within itself. For it is not so much that you are within the cosmos as that the cosmos is within you.

✸

BODY AND FOOD

THE physical body cannot exist without food, and therefore in an indirect sense they are one and the same. The body assimilates that portion of the food which is useful for its maintenance, and throws out that portion which is useless. That which is discarded is as much part of the food that was consumed as that which is assimilated. If man is so supremely indifferent to the eliminated refuse, why should he not feel the same detachment towards the assimilated food which, for practical purposes, becomes his body? Why should he shed tears when, after death, the body itself is cast off to the care of earthworms or to consuming flames?

REAL UNTOUCHABLES

THE real untouchables are those who cannot enter the temple of their own hearts and see the Lord therein.

WORLD PEACE

EVERYWHERE today man is rightfully occupied with the problem of world peace. If there is war, it means nothing short of racial suicide and total destruction. But world peace cannot be ensured through dogmas, however learned, or organizations, however efficient. It can be ensured only by a release of unarguing and unconquerable love which knows no fear or separateness.

Humanity is not going to be saved by any material power — nuclear or otherwise. It can be saved only through divine intervention. God has never failed humanity in its dark and critical periods. The greatest danger to man today is not from any natural catastrophe, but from himself.

It is not possible to realize human brotherhood merely by appealing to high ideals or to a sense of duty. Something more than that is essential to release human consciousness from the clutches of selfishness and greed.

Today the urgent need of mankind is not sects or organized religions, but LOVE. Divine love will conquer hate and fear. It will not depend upon other justifications, but will justify itself.

I have come to awaken in man this divine love. It will restore to him the unfathomable richness of his own eternal being and will solve all of his problems.

BEGIN TO LOVE GOD*

THE youth of today is the ruling force of to-morrow. All things have a small beginning: the seedling grows into a tree, the stream into a river, and the child grows into a man to use or misuse the lessons he has absorbed in life as a youth. But even after he has grown into a man he often remains a child in the spiritual sense of the word. The world is the kindergarten and school necessary for the spiritual lessons man must learn through countless lives of experiencing the opposites such as pain and pleasure, joy and suffering, good and bad, wealth and poverty.

All growth is gradual, and it is only through slow and gradual stages that man truly begins to "grow up" and discover his true Self, and to relinquish the childish playthings of hate, greed and anger through selfless service and love. In the spiritual school also there are many grades to be passed, for which few have the required courage and determination. Just as there are masters and instructors to guide you along the path of your studies, so there are Perfect Mas-

* Baba gave this as a spiritual message for young people.

ters who can guide you along the path of the spirit to the glorious destination of Godhood. Few have the good fortune to meet and follow such a spiritual guide, — when you do, you must earn his grace and be worthy of his love.

Do not balk at the discipline given by your parents and teachers. Discipline in small ways leads to the greater necessary discipline of Self. Do not try to conquer others — conquer yourself and you will have conquered the world. The simplest way to do this is to love God. Begin to love God by loving your fellow beings. Begin to see God by seeing Him in all beings and things. Give without thought of return, serve without thought of reward. God is everywhere, in everything. Most of all He is right within yourself. You do not exist for the world — the world exists for you.

There is an amusing illustration of this in the story of the ant. An ant was trying to cross a stream on a leaf. Tossed by the wind, the leaf overturned in midstream and the ant cried, "Help, help, the world is drowning."

A frog close by said, "What rubbish! The world is not drowning, you mean *you* are drowning."

"Well," said the ant, "once I drown the world might as well not exist for me, so for me it means not only that I am drowning but that the world is drowning too!"

In the same way, all existence is within you. God is to be found within yourself, and once you find Him you have found the only treasure worth finding. I give you my blessing that you may love God and find Him.

ALL IS FROM WITHIN

ALL achievements, through progress in science or otherwise, are but superficial explorations of that which is without. If that which is within be realized, the root of all that is without is made bare, and man will experience that everything emerges from within him as the shadow of his infinite Self.

GOD IS IN ALL

IN THE divine scales, vice and virtue are necessary experiences man goes through before attaining the supreme balance of Self-realization, which is beyond all opposites — good and bad.

"Good" is like a clean mirror that reflects the image of God. When true knowledge is gained you realize that the reflection is the image of your own Self, the GOD that is in all and in everything.

"Bad" is like the dusty particles that accumulate and hide the image of God, until the mirror presents only a distorted or blank surface. It cannot affect the object being reflected; it merely distorts your vision.

LOVE is the cleanser that wipes the mirror bright and enables you to behold with increasing clarity the indivisible Entity that permeates all life.

The negative experience of the "bad," with its consequent suffering, ultimately disgusts man and leads him to the positive force of "good," thus awakening divine love. Hence, the saints of the present are the sinners of the past. In the clarity of the understanding and knowledge they have gained they show true humility. They do not take pride in their achievements nor condemn the "sinner" whom they know to belong equally to God, but help him to remove the self-created veil of ignorance and perceive his true identity.

Man cannot escape his glorious destiny of Self-realization, and no amount of suffering that he passes through on the way to it can ever be too much. After the apex of suffering has been reached, the time will soon come for mankind to have a deeper spiritual understanding, bringing it closer together in universal love and brotherhood in the bond of divine knowledge — the only knowledge worth having.

General Messages to Mankind

THE TWO

THERE are two who do not have any use for religion: the materialist and the one who is Self-realized. There are two who are indifferent to money: the sot and the one who is Self-realized. There are two who are free from lust: the child and the one who has attained Truth.

Though the Truth-realized person appears to be similar in the above respects to the materialist, the sot and the child, he stands completely apart from all these. He has attained unity with the infinite existence of God, while the others have not.

DIVINE LOVE AND WINE

DIVINE love and wine are both distant from the creeds of established religion; the former is beyond the creeds and the latter is disapproved of by them. Both are intoxicating and make man forgetful. But while wine leads to self-oblivion, divine love leads to self-knowledge.

KNOWLEDGE THROUGH EXPERIENCE

THE knowledge of Truth as gained through the established creeds is like the knowledge of a town which one gets by studying it on a map. To see and know the town one has to take the trouble of actually going there.

It is one thing merely to see the picture of a cow; quite a different thing to have a real cow and to drink its milk.

In the same way all religious creeds, though useful for the time being, ultimately must be replaced by actual experience and the inner spiritual Path must be traversed before one can realize the infinite Truth.

LABOR OF LOVE*

THE source of eternal bliss is the Self in all. The cause of perpetual misery is the selfishness of all. As long as satisfaction is derived through selfish pursuits, misery will always exist.

*Baba gave this answer to the following question asked of him on television:

"Why should misery perpetually exist on earth in spite of God's infinite love and mercy?" [The Editor]

Only because of the infinite love and mercy of God can man learn to realize, through the lessons of misery on earth, that inherent in him is the source of infinite bliss, and all suffering is his labor of love to unveil his own infinte Self.

WILL-O'-THÉ-WISP

Look at your own shadow. It seems so near to you. It is adjoining you, but you cannot grasp it nor overtake it in a race. You may chase your shadow till doomsday, but it will still evade you and remain a bit ahead of you.

Seeking God through the ego-mind is like trying to overtake your own shadow. It cannot be done, not because God is in any way far off, but because you can never get the real through the false. The real is gained only when the false is given up.

God is nearer to you than your own shadow. In fact, He is not only within you, but He is your very self. You cannot get at Him, for you seek Him through the ego-mind which converts Him into the will-o'-the-wisp. The ego-mind must meet actual death if God is to be seen and realized.

PANORAMA OF SOUL CONSCIOUSNESS

Phase	Form	Gross	Subtle	Mental	Se
Evolution	Mineral	Minute	Nil	Nil	Ni
"	Vegetable	Little	Nil	Nil	Ni
"	Animal	More	Nil	Nil	Ni
"	Man	Full	Nil	Nil	Ni
Involution	Advanced man (in subtle sphere)	Nil	Full	Nil	Ni
"	More advanced man (in mental sphere)	Nil	Nil	Full	Ni
Man as God		Nil	Nil	Nil	Fu
Mastery	Man as God and man	Full	Full	Full	Fu
Mastery in Servitude	God as Man	Simultaneously consciou of one and all individual and collective phases.			

God being infinitely infinite and indivisible, nothing can exist without Him and outside of Him; hence, unknown to you, God is also in your "I Am"-ness of duality. Since God is in you and you are in God, where can the gross, subtle and mental spheres exist but in your own existence?

Just as consciousness remains latent in a man sleeping soundly, *full* consciousness remains latent in the soul. At first it begins to manifest or evolve through flickering dreams, sound asleep and awakening, and successive experiences in the mineral, vegetable and animal kingdoms of the gross sphere, until it reaches the stage of man where consciousness is full and complete.

Though consciousness is fully manifested in man it remains wedged between the necessary opposite experiences of duality. Knowingly or unknowingly man is always trying to free it in order to be able to direct it towards his own true Self.

Be it minute, little, more or full; be it gross, subtle, mental or of the Self, the soul's consciousness is the beginning and the end in a beginningless and endless panorama of God's infinitude, and through it you realize your own infinite power, immeasurable knowledge and unfathomable bliss.

FROM TRIPLICITY TO UNITY

THE Eternal Truth has three aspects: *Dnyana* or knowledge, *Shakti* or power and *Ananda* or bliss. The *Sakshatkara* or the realization of this three-fold Divinity or Truth is the target of the seeker. Those who take the path of *Prem* or love bask in eternal joy. Those who are on the path of action take refuge in eternal power. Persons who seek wisdom rely on eternal knowledge.

But at the end of the Path, all have to come to the indivisible completeness of the Truth, in all its aspects, however different their paths may have been. One who arrives at the Goal is the Truth-realized individual, and he becomes the very Source of infinite knowledge, infinite power and infinite bliss.

ETERNAL NOW

THROUGH enslavement to the temporary and the passing, man deprives himself of the eternal and the lasting. Each moment with which man is confronted can either tighten the grip of the false or deliver him to the Truth. God is the only Reality and He is the fountainhead of all love, beauty, peace and happiness. Even in and through the "fleeting now" of the false, God is eternally inviting man to Himself, affirming Himself as the Truth of man's being. Those who dare to see and love God in everyone and everything, experience Him as the everlastingly immediate Presence.

Only when his mind is utterly detached from the false is it possible for man to disentangle himself from the repetitive clutches of the fleeting moment. Then and only then can he become established in the "eternal now," which everlastingly includes the eternal past and the eternal future. The eternal "I Am" is an unfailing assurance of the only Reality which ever was, is and will be.

The way to peace and fulfillment in union with God, the divine Beloved, is a daring dive into the "eternal now." Not by fruitless surveys of the past, nor by elusive longings for the future, nor by enslavement to the fleeting moment, but by staking everything for God, is it possible for you to experience yourself as the illimitable ocean of love. Here and nowhere else is the final solution of all your problems. Love born in the Truth liberates without binding and fulfills without overpowering; it is a pure blessing not only for yourself, but for each and all, for ever and ever, in the "eternal now."

THE DIVINE UNION

Not through worldly wisdom, but by diving deep to the innermost, is it possible to be united with God, Who is at once the Lover and the Beloved. For this union, one must summon the necessary courage to rise beyond the alluring shadows of the illusory world of sense-perception. Consciousness, loaded with attachments, gets pinned to the sense-world of duality. Mere withdrawal of consciousness from the world of forms presents a vacuum of nothing. But when consciousness is illumined by the Truth, it reveals God as everything and it experiences one uninterrupted and endless continuity of limitless bliss, love, power and understanding.

THE FINAL ACCOUNT

WHEN the goal of life is attained, one achieves the reparation of all wrongs, the healing of all wounds, the righting of all failures, the sweetening of all sufferings, the relaxation of all strivings, the harmonizing of all strife, the unraveling of all enigmas, and the real and full meaning of all life — past, present and future.

Meher Baba and His Activities

THE INVIOLABLE UNITY
OF LIFE

IT IS my God-ordained work to awaken humanity to the inviolable unity and inalienable divinity of all life. Know that you are in essence eternal, and heirs to infinite knowledge, bliss and power. In order to enjoy your unlimited state, all that is necessary is to shed your ignorance which makes you feel that you are separate from the rest of life. The separative ego or "I" can disappear only through divine love, which will be my gift to mankind.

Let those who hearken to my call prepare themselves to render real service to mankind. Let them make it conscious of its oneness, irrespective of the apparent divisions of class, sect or creed. I do not attach importance to beliefs or dogmas. It is not what you *believe* but what you *are* that will ultimately count.

The Truth which I want you to share with me is not a matter of opinion or belief but of direct experience which knows no contradiction, and which will make you realize that nothing in this world is worth being greedy about, and that there need not be any hatred, jealousy or fear. Then, and only then, will man launch himself upon the safe voyage of unending creativity and unfading happiness which knows no decay or fear; he will have transcended the duality of "I" and "you," "mine" and "thine."

RELIGION

THOUGH religion has come into existence to liberate man from all narrowness, it can itself become a cage when not understood properly. All the world religions proclaim the same eternal and universal Truth; yet human weakness has a tendency to carve out some limiting, narrow loyalty which closes its gates upon the shoreless and unbounded ocean of love or divinity. It is not the essentials of religions, but addiction merely to their outer forms, which has tended to divide man from man, thus thwarting the very purpose of the great founders of the world religions.

I invite man to break through all of his self-created prisons, and taste of the unlimited life which I bring. I ask him to love divinely, fear-lessly and limitlessly and to rise above the limited self of the separative ego-mind. I come to impart to groping humanity the universal Truth which transcends sectarian divisions and dogmatic formulations.

Through ages of darkness and suffering man-kind awaits me and my Truth. I and the Truth which I bring are inseparable, one from the other. I am one with the Truth. May you all, too, break through the numberless cages and realize that you are one with the limitless Truth of divine life. The divine Beloved is always with you, in you and around you. Know that you are not separate from Him.

DIVINE LIFE

THE silence which I have been observing for the past thirty-one years is not intended to veil my Truth but to manifest it. When you realize the Truth as the very core of your being you are free from all fear and helplessness, and all rivalries and conflicts reveal themselves to be meaningless, for you know yourself to be inviolably one with all that has life.

To the struggling, failing and faltering humanity I say, "Have faith." Turn to God in complete surrenderance and receive the divine love. You are equally a part of the one indivisible divine life. There is not a single atom that does not vibrate with this divine life.

There is no need for anyone to despair. The greatest of sinners as well as the greatest of saints has the same unfailing divine assurance.

HOW DOES ONE WORK FOR BABA?

WORK undertaken with honest intent and love for God is Baba's work, and those who do this are always his.

But the greatest work one can do for Baba is to live the life of love, humility, sincerity and selfless service in which there is no trace of hypocrisy. Baba's love is for all; and for each of his lovers to help others know this, his or her own life must be a radiating example of love so that it may become the instrument to spread

Baba's love and the truth of Reality. Such a life and such a love are vital and carry the highest responsibility, for behind every thought, word and deed is the all-pervading force of Truth.

To cultivate discipline in one's self requires self-determination and honest effort if one desires to tread knowingly and consciously the path of love. This discipline may at first appear dry as dust, but with perseverance it will automatically blossom and be transmuted into the very life of the lover.

To help others through one's own example, one must get not only thoroughly drenched but drowned in love. As a prelude one should attempt to create a balance between the thoughts of the mind and the feelings of the heart. Mind, however, works much faster. Thoughts are like lightning — first there is the flash and later the sound of thunder. For an equilibrium to be reached, the mind — which is the seat of desires — must be made to function more slowly in order to keep pace with the heart, and no amount of silence or fasting can accomplish this.

If the individual desires the enforcement of equilibrium in the true direction, a consistent acceleration of feelings should be made so that feelings supersede thoughts, *i.e.*, the heart supersedes the mind. To achieve this the only effective fuel is love — unadulterated love. Unless one learns to love in its true sense, one cannot cross the hurdle of the mind. And for one to understand love in its true sense, the only recourse is to dedicate one's self to the Lord of love, and to hold fast under all circumstances to the feet of the Perfect Master. Any deviation from self-dedication will lead one astray from the path of divine love.

It is good to fast and observe silence as a discipline in one's daily life. But this becomes utterly insignificant when one has determined to starve and silence the mind itself, by implicitly obeying in all things a Sadguru — a Perfect Master.

Baba's love is with his lovers always, helping and guiding them. And they? They should keep their love for him alive and aglow, by making him their constant companion in all their thoughts, words and actions, while carrying on their responsibilities, commitments and all other apparently necessary things of this world, though these have no foundation of their own in the domain of Reality.

BABA ON HIS ACTIVITIES

MAN, becoming God, achieves perfection; but when man, after consciously becoming God, returns to gross consciousness as man, he has achieved the supreme perfection. Such a Perfect Master is not only God, but lives the life of God as man. Perfection does not merely mean escaping from the Mayavic law. The Perfect Master is in Maya and simultaneously beyond it. He is amidst the law of karma but not bound by it. Whatever his actions, they are non-actions, for the actions which bind ordinary man are not only non-binding when performed by the Perfect Master, but are channels for his universal spiritual work of liberating mankind from the ignorance of Maya. The Perfect Masters are free from freedom itself, and so are free even from the non-actions that they perform for their universal work.

To those who wish to know about my activities I can only say that as far as my inner life and internal activities are concerned, only God and those who are one with God can know and understand. As far as my external activities are concerned regarding my work with the God-intoxicated, saints, "sadhus" and the poor; of contacting them, working with them, serving them and bowing down to them in devotion, they have all been recorded by a disciple of mine in *The Wayfarers*.*

I enjoy games, chiefly cricket, playing marbles, flying kites and also listening to music, although I can do so only on rare occasions. From time immemorial, I have been playing with the Mayavic universe and this enjoyment of playing still persists. I sometimes see motion pictures (mostly humorous ones), and enjoy my real state of being the eternal Producer of the vast, ever-changing, never-ending film called the universe. I also find relaxation in listening to humorous stories, all the time being aware of the humor that lies in the aspect of the soul, which is the source of infinite power and glory, being made to feel so helpless in its human bondage of ignorance arising from its various forms of duality.

I allow vegetarians to follow their diet and non-vegetarians to eat meat, fish, etc. However, those who stay with me have as a rule vegetarian diet according to my instructions, unless

* By William Donkin.

on occasion I instruct otherwise. Once in a great while I give wine to my lovers and make them understand that it is not this wine of grapes but the pure wine of love, giving divine intoxication, that helps towards union with God.

I do not interfere with any religion and permit all to follow unhindered their own creeds. When compared with love for God, external ceremonials have no value. Love for God automatically and naturally results in self-denial, mental control and ego-annihilation, irrespective of the lovers' following or renouncing these external forms.

Once in a while I give "darshan" and "prasad" of love to the people, each person benefiting according to his or her own receptivity. I give "updesh" (spiritual advice) in the form of instructions to those who are closely connected with me. Perfect Masters can impart divine knowledge, bestow divine love and shower the grace of God-union by a mere glance, touch or single divine thought.

From the beginningless beginning to the present day I Am What I Am, irrespective of praise or universal opposition, and will remain so to the endless end.

DIVINE BLISS AND HUMAN
SUFFERING

"How CAN the individualized soul that continually experiences infinite bliss suffer bodily ailments and be susceptible to ordinary heat and cold?" one may ask.

It is true that illusory things, one and all, individual and collective, local and universal, cease to exist even as illusion when man once becomes God-realized, the Perfect One, eternally conscious of his own infinite Oneness. Whether the gross, subtle and mental bodies of such a Perfect One remain or drop, they Do Not Exist for him. There is nothing in illusion that exists for him — yet he exists for all things within the illusion of ignorance and his abundantly overflowing Godhood takes care of them, including his body. Until dropped, the physical body of the Perfect One remains immune to ailments, and is unaffected by heat or cold because these are automatically neutralized through his own all-pervading God-consciousness.

A Perfect One very rarely becomes a Perfect Master, as did St. Francis of Assisi, returning *with* God-consciousness to the realm of illusion. When he does, he is fully conscious of his physical body and of one and all the spheres of illusory existence, without experiencing a break in the infinite bliss of the indivisible Oneness of his being.

In short, the God-realized or Perfect One has God-consciousness with no consciousness whatever of anything else, as nothing other than God exists for him. The Perfect Master has God-consciousness plus consciousness of illusion.

It is the complete and absolute unconsciousness of his body (as of all other illusory things) that keeps the body of the Perfect One untouched by environmental conditions and effects, whereas it is the regaining of consciousness of the body which makes the Perfect Master susceptible to its ordinary ailments and sufferings.

Not only do Perfect Masters not use their divine power to avoid or alleviate their own physical suffering which they consciously experience as illusion, but they take upon themselves physical suffering in order to alleviate the spiritual ignorance of others who are in the bondage of illusion. St. Francis of Assisi suffered such excruciating headaches that he had to dash his head against stone, although others could be healed by the touch of his hand. Jesus Christ suffered the tortures of crucifixion to take on the suffering of the universe. Being simultaneously the Father and Son, His own infinite bliss was not interrupted by the cross nor did this status intervene in the bodily agony which He suffered as an ordinary human being. The sublime difference in individual suffering lies in the fact that an ordinary man suffers for himself, Masters suffer for humanity, and the Avatar suffers for one and all beings and things.*

---

*Baba gave this explanation to the above question that had arisen in the minds of a few after his auto accident in the U. S. A. in 1952 when he underwent severe bodily injury. To quote extracts from the report of Dr. Goher Irani, who was among the disciples following in another car at the time of the accident: "Baba's face and left side of the body were badly injured, resulting in fractures of the left humerus and left tibia and fibula. The nose was severely damaged, the nasal bone being fractured and displaced and the septum markedly deflected causing profuse bleeding from the nose. As a result the structural appearance of the nose is considerably altered. The mucous membrane of the nose and accessory sinuses have become very sensitive and prone to congestion with the slightest exposure to cold, causing orbital and frontal headaches, heaviness and fullness in the nose, and puffiness under the eyelids. This condition is aggravated during damp weather and winter months."

As Avatar, the bodily suffering Baba takes upon himself is a significant part of his work and Baba has not let it interfere with other aspects of his work. With the hindrance of his leg in a plaster cast and arm in a sling Baba saw hundreds of people in America, England and Switzerland. On his return to India, before he had scarcely given up the use of his crutches, Baba carried out a whirlwind tour of mass darshans in the north and south of India — traveling thousands of miles, visiting numerous towns and villages, dictating over a hundred messages on the alphabet board and personally distributing "prasad" of sweets and fruit to some fifteen thousand men, women and children at a time. This kind of rigorous activity Baba has kept up at frequent intervals since then, regardless of the physical exertion involved, alternating intermittently with periods of seclusion and fasting. The universal spiritual work done by Baba during his seclusion left in its wake a complete exhaustion of the *human* aspects of his mind and body. But his work went on, and Baba told us that his visit to the West in the midst of his 1955-1956 seclusion was of momentous significance. [The Editor]

THE AVATAR'S ADVENT

AGE after age the Avatar comes amidst mankind to maintain his own creation of illusion, thereby also awakening humanity to awareness of it. The framework of illusion is always one and the same, but the designs in illusion are innumerable and ever-changing. My advent is not to destroy illusion because illusion, as it is, is absolutely nothing. I come to make you become aware of the nothingness of illusion. Through you I automatically maintain illusion which is nothing but the shadow of my infinite Self, and through me you automatically discard illusion when you experience its falseness.

MEHER BABA

Meher Baba dropped his body on January 31, 1969. The final years of his physical presence were spent in close seclusion marked by painfully intense and exhausting preoccupation with his universal work. In 1968 he announced this had been completed to *his* 100 percent satisfaction. The same period also witnessed the prairie-fire growth in numbers of those who looked to him for the key to meaning in life. Thousands of these passed before the well-loved form as it lay for seven days in the tomb at Meherabad near Ahmednagar, India. More thousands from all over the world attended the April-to-June darshan he had arranged months before. The impact of these occasions on the inner man, and of the months that have now gone by, bear witness to the force of love set in motion by the one we have known and accepted to be the Avatar of our time.